MW00534878

TURNING
BOXES
WITH
FRICTION-FITTED
LIDS

Bill Bowers

Schiffer *Publishing Ltd* ®

4880 Lower Valley Road • Atglen, PA 19310

Dedication

To: Burt Biss, sage, intellectual, advisor, counselor, confidant, purveyor of Oregon timber, and someone who enjoys comestible fare I create and fine wines.

Contents

Other Schiffer Books by Bill Bowers

The Basics of Turning Spirals,
ISBN: 0-7643-2592-2, $14.95

10 Easy Turning Projects for the Smaller Lathe,
ISBN: 978-0-7643-2727-8, $14.95

7 Great Turning Projects for the Smaller Lathe,
ISBN: 978-0-7643-2726-1, $14.95

Copyright © 2008 by William Bowers
Library of Congress Control Number: 2008921040

Designed by Stephanie Daugherty
Type set in Zurich/Zurich

ISBN: 978-0-7643-3027-8
Printed in China

Schiffer Books are available at special discounts for bulk purchases for sales promotions or premiums. Special editions, including personalized covers, corporate imprints, and excerpts can be created in large quantities for special needs. For more information contact the publisher:

Published by Schiffer Publishing Ltd.
4880 Lower Valley Road
Atglen, PA 19310
Phone: (610) 593-1777; Fax: (610) 593-2002
E-mail: Info@schifferbooks.com

For the largest selection of fine reference books on this and related subjects, please visit our website at
www.schifferbooks.com
We are always looking for people to write books on new and related subjects. If you have an idea for a book, please contact us at proposals@schifferbooks.com

This book may be purchased from the publisher.
Please try your bookstore first.
You may write for a free catalog.

Proem

There has been a multitude of books, VHS tapes, and DVDs produced on how to turn boxes. So many in fact, that another text on the subject may seem somewhat redundant. Nevertheless, a quick perusal through this brief and well illustrated text will entice the reader to try the projects and prove the initial premise incorrect. Even though watching a DVD may be the best means of learning for many, dust laden workshops prove insalubrious to fine electronic equipment. A well illustrated, caption driven text is the best alternative.

The turned box projects described herein are selected so that beginning to intermediate turners may readily master the techniques, using each of the previously described box projects as the basis for their expertise. The projects tend to be fun, rewarding, and satisfying. I still recall my first professional class with Ray Key, where we made some of the boxes illustrated.

There really is nothing new in turning boxes. Many individuals have tried all sorts of permutations and combinations, but the basic idea of structure and form remains the same with only a few variations. Due credit is noted to those particular individuals who have signature boxes associated with their name.

Throughout the book one will see many repetitions in constructing boxes. The processes are similar in turning all forms with only minor alterations to create different structures. The processes in sanding and finishing are the same throughout.

The logical beginning is an explanation of how to turn a cylinder box. It is the simplest to turn but requires adequate skill to make it flawless. It is a great exercise in tooling and touch. The second chapter illustrates some cylinder box variants and how to construct more complicated forms. Chapter three demonstrates how to make a useful travel capsule box, while chapter four describes some capsule box variants with chatter tool embellishments. Chapter five illustrates construction of the classic Raffan type box and chapter six goes into great detail in constructing the complicated pagoda box of Ray Key. Chapter seven discusses how to use left over or scrap box material to make clam shell boxes. Chapter eight illustrates construction of the Stuart Batty pumpkin or gourd box. Chapter nine details the bottle top and finial top hollow form boxes of Ray Key. The last chapter is a gallery of boxes, provided to stimulate the imagination and entice turners to try some of their own creations.

Because of the book's layout it is suggested the reader start at chapter one, working their way through successive chapters to gain the skills and confidence to tackle more difficult projects in succeeding chapters. The tools needed are standard turning tools, except for a few that have be modified or ground for special tasks. They are all described and illustrated in the text. A large lathe is not needed to make boxes. In fact, all the projects may be made on a mini-lathe.

A brief word needs to be expressed on friction fitted boxes. The friction fit should be tight enough for the box to be lifted by its lid without the base falling off. In other words, one should have to use both hands to open the box. If one lives in a dry climate most of the seasoned wood will be dry from that climate. (If one is using exotics one must remember that it takes 12 to 15 years for them to dry.) Making a tight fitting lid will yield a stable box. However, if one lives in a dry climate and is producing boxes to be shipped to a damp climate either for retail sales or as gifts, a different scenario ensues. The fitted lid must be turned loose or else the recipient will never be able to remove it. Placing the box in a freezer will allow initial removal but the lid will never fit again. The reverse is true for those living in damp climates shipping to a dry climate. The fit must be extremely tight and still the lid may become loose upon arrival. If one lives in a climate like Alaska where the relative humidity may be 10% in the winter and 80% in the summer there is no solution except threaded lids.

Chapter 1
The Cylinder Box

The cylinder box is probably one of the easiest, as well as simplest, to construct, and, if accomplished with great care and dexterity, one of the best to hone one's skills in turning boxes. It is a project with which all new box makers should begin. Even an experienced box maker may learn to polish his craft by paying attention to the suggested details herein.

Principles to be remembered are the correct proportions of stock thickness to height, lid to base, wall thickness, and care in finishing all surfaces. Remembering the golden mean (1.6180339887 or phi, a number that goes to infinity without repeating and a ratio utilized throughout art and architecture) will give the most pleasing proportions to the eye.

Some suggest the ratio of 2/5 to 3/5 as the proper portions or in some instances 1/3 to 2/3. If one calculates out the golden mean the percentage is 0.618 as opposed to 0.6 for 3/5 or 0.667 for 2/3.

Another important factor is selection of the proper timber for the box. A domestic hardwood will take tooling rather easily and is amiable to a nice friction-fitted junction. Exotics, although they are most appealing to the eye, are much more difficult to turn, tool, and finish. The tool angle for cutting must be more obtuse with the burr removed after sharpening. For the neophyte with aggressive turning tendencies, catches are common. Burl on the other hand, may yield rather lovely completed pieces and be much easier to manage.

The selected timber is amboyna burl (the burl found on the Papua New Guinea rosewood tree or Narra). It is dense, requiring tooling with very sharp edges. The stock is 2-3/4 inches by 4-1/2 inches. The corners have been carefully cut off on a band saw using a fine-toothed blade (1/4 inch, 12 tpi). By converting the square stock to a semi-round piece, the problem of fracturing dense timbers with the roughing gouge is resolved. The stock is mounted between centers using a 7/8 inch Steb center and Oneway live center and then turned to a cylinder at 2000 rpms using a sharpened, 1-1/4 inch Ashley Iles roughing gouge. Square the ends using a diamond parting tool.

After measuring the 1-1/2 inch opening of the O'Donnell jaws, mark the measurement on both ends of the stock. Remember to touch only one point of the dividers in making the mark.

Use the diamond parting tool to cut a 1/8 inch spigot at each end to fit the Axminster's O'Donnell jaws. The top of the jaws should rest against the bottom of the cylinder so that the stock is held in 2 perpendicular supporting planes.

4

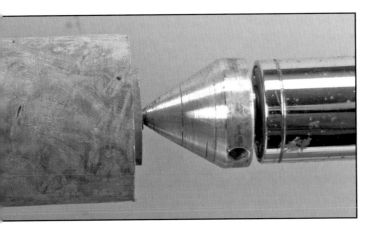

Mount the stock into the O'Donnell jaws. If any irregularity is noted with rotation, touch up the cylinder with the roughing gouge—because of the propensity of this particular burl to chip, a skew chisel would not be the tool of choice. Mark on the base of the stock pencil marks and on the jaws, red Sharpie marks, so that the same mount position may be used later on.

Measure the distance for the lid (1-1/2 inches) and base (2-1/2 inches) and mark with a red pencil line.

Retract the tailstock live center before parting off the lid. Some may wish to use a dovetail or dowel saw to do this, but the parting tool may be used as well if the turner carefully captures the parted lid before it hits the floor or lathe.

Mount the parted lid in the O'Donnell jaws by its spigot. Use the 1/2 inch skew to square the cut surface.

Using the depth gauge, mark the depth to give a thickness of 1/4 inch for the lid's top—if we were turning a smaller box a thickness of 3/16 inches would be used.

Use a modified 1/2 inch spindle gouge (the Ray Key hollowing tool) to hollow out the lid. Remember to keep the flute closed as the center point is drilled and the tool tip is swept out towards the sides of the cylinder. Hollow the lid to a flat bottom and straight sides with a 1/4 inch thickness. There should be a subtle curve at the junction of the inside lid and cylindrical interior wall.

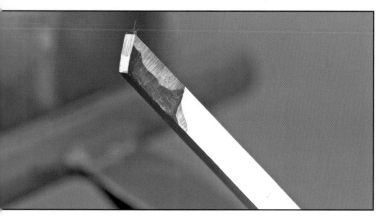

Notice the detail of the 1/4 inch square rebate tool sharpened to a 70 degree angle at its tip and 60 degrees along its left side back about 3/4 inches. This tool is used to cut the female portion of the friction fit. You may carefully use it to push in or cut from the interior to the side to prevent catches. Remember to remove the burr from sharpening with a fine diamond card, especially when turning exotics.

Use a square-nose scrapper after rounding the corner to finish the bottom and sides of the interior.

Cut the rebate one-half the thickness (1/8 inch) of the wall and about 1/4 inch deep. The angle of attack is 30 degrees, as noted, to prevent catches. The cut portion of the interior wall should match the cut spigot of the base so that the interior walls in the finished product are as straight and parallel as the outside walls.

Remember to scrape with the tool angled as shown. If a catch should happen the tool will be pushed out of the way. If one holds the tool parallel to the lathe bed or scrapes upward a catch will destroy the piece with a giant dig-in.

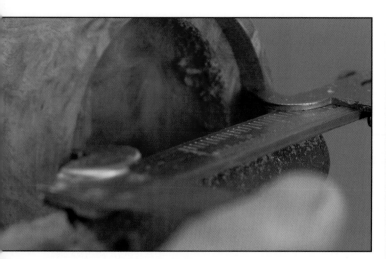

With calipers, check the rebate walls to make sure they are straight and square to the perpendicular surfaces.

With the tip of the 1/2 inch skew, cut concentric circles for a design element.

Finish sanding with 150 to 400 grit waxed sandpaper (this cuts down on dust and heat as well as creating a sanding sealer). If your lathe has a reverse setting, reverse directions between grits. Remember not to sand the cut rebate, as this will round over the fit, preventing good gripping of the lid to base. Buff with #0000 waxed steel wool, brush on diluted lacquer (Deft cut in half with lacquer thinner), friction dry the lacquer with a soft cloth, and then apply a finish wax such as Briwax.

Remount the base in the O'Donnell jaws using the previously made mounting position marks.

With dividers set slightly proud of the rebate's opening, make a circular mark on the base. Remember to touch only one point of the dividers.

Use the 1/4 inch rebate tool to carefully cut down to the divider marks.

Check the fit of the lid. By cutting only a small spigot, you leave some room for adjustment if the fit is too loose and the end needs to be turned off to start again.

Once the proper fit is reached, extend the spigot to 1/4 inch to fit into the lid. The fit has to be tight enough to allow the lid's top to be turned to completion. There will also be some loosening of the lid once the base is hollowed out. Cut a 1/32 inch wide x 1/32 inch deep defining mark between lid and base.

Using a 3/8-inch spindle gouge turn off the spigot on the lid's top.

Use the 1/2-inch skew to cut a subtle curve, leaving an exterior rim.

Use the skew's tip to cut concentric circles for a design.

Finish by sanding with waxed sandpaper 150 to 400 grits and #0000 waxed steel wool. Apply diluted lacquer and friction dry it, then apply Briwax as was done before.

With a narrow parting tool, mark the box bottom extension.

Next use the Ray Key hollowing tool to hollow out the interior bottom as was done for the lid. Remember, this tool needs to be applied at dead center with the flute closed as demonstrated.

Measure the depth to make sure the bottom will be 1/4 inch thick.

Using the rounded corner square-nose scraper, finish the interior bottom and sides. The spigot should measure 1/8 inch thick and 1/4 inch deep to squarely fit the lid.

Finish the interior with waxed sandpaper 150 to 400 grits, #0000 waxed steel wool, diluted lacquer friction dried, and Briwax.

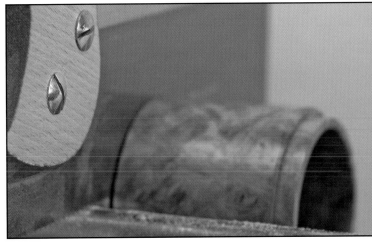

Use the narrow parting tool to cut a 1/2 inch diameter dowel to be cut off with the dovetail saw. If one tries to part off the base with the narrow parting tool sometimes the thinness of the base will allow a blowout hole, especially with end grain turning.

Remove the left-over amboyna burl and save it for another project, then mount some softer scrap timber in the O'Donnell jaws. Cut a spigot and fit on the base so that the bottom may be finished.

Turn off the spigot and cut a subtle concavity with the 1/2-inch skew.

9

Using the point of the skew, cut several concentric circles for design.

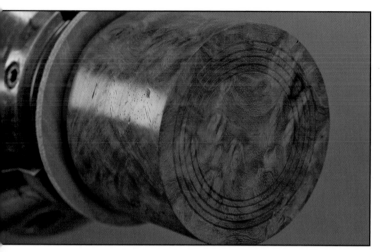

Finish the bottom by sanding 150 to 400 grits, apply a diluted lacquer which is friction dried, and then apply wax.

The finished box of amboyna burl.

Notice the fine detail of the box top and bottom.

Detail of the interior of top and bottom pieces.

Chapter 2
The Cylinder Box Variants

The classic cylinder box has many variants but only two will be described in this chapter. The same procedures and principles are utilized in their construction, with only a few modifications. The variants are basically embellishments turned on the cylinder boxes.

After band sawing off the corners of the stock, mounting between centers to turn a cylinder with the roughing gouge, marking out the golden mean ratios for lid and base, and turning the mounting spigots, a ringed lip embellished cylinder box is ready for construction.

A rounded piece of tambootie, 2-3/4 inches diameter x 3-1/2 inches tall, with the lid and base layout and beginning bead between the top and bottom junction, shows the beginning of the box. A defining cut with the narrow parting tool has been made to better appreciate the beginning 1/8 inch thick bead.

Using a 3/8-inch spindle gouge, further define the bead and cut down the top diameter so that the ledge created is about 3/16 inches deep and 1/8 inch thick.

Mount the stock by the previously cut spigot in 2-inch O'Donnell jaws. Use the 1/2-inch skew to evenly cut the sides of the lid and correct any irregularity in circumference.

Use the 3/8-inch spindle gouge to cut down the base, then use the skew to square the base to the lid. Remove the tailstock and part off the lid.

Mount the lid by its spigot and square the cut surface with the skew.

Begin to hollow the top using the modified 1/2-inch spindle gouge as was done on the simple cylinder box. Don't forget to measure with the depth gauge to a wall thickness of 3/16 inches. You must also account for the beaded rim's depth in figuring the wall thickness (3/16 plus 3/16, or 3/8 inches, thick at the ring)

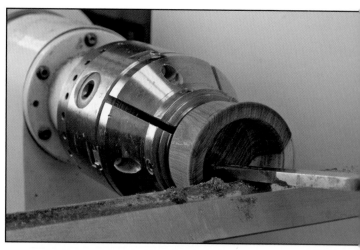

Using the rounded corner square-nose scraper, flatten the interior lid and square the sides. Remember to scrape at a 30 degree angle and remove the burr off the tool tip after sharpening.

Use the 1/4-inch square modified rebate tool to cut a 1/4 inch deep x 3/32 inches wide rebate.

With the tip of the 1/2-inch skew, cut concentric circles on the interior of the lid for design.

Sand with 150 to 400 grit waxed sandpaper, reversing directions with each grit, and finish with #0000 waxed steel wool, thinned friction-dried lacquer, and Briwax.

Remove the lid and measure slightly proud of the opening with dividers.

Remount the base using the previously made marks for the same position as the original was turned. Make the divider marks touching only one point on the skew squared surface.

Use the rebate tool to cut the 1/4 inch wide spigot.

Check the fit to make sure it is tight, as it will loosen when the base is hollowed.

Use the 3/8-inch spindle gouge to turn off and flatten the top of the lid. Use the skew to make a subtle curve with an end ridge and concentric circles for design.

Complete the lid by sanding with waxed sandpaper 150 to 400 grits, #0000 waxed steel wool, and apply the diluted lacquer (friction-dried) and Briwax.

Mount the base on a turned jam chuck to finish it. Turn off the spigot with the 3/8-inch spindle gouge.

Remove the lid and hollow out the base to a wall thickness of 3/16 inches, then use the square nose scraper to flatten the interior base and walls. The finished spigot should be 3/32 inches thick to match the interior diameter of the lid.

Use the skew to make concentric circles for design, then apply the finishing touches.

Finish by sanding with waxed sandpaper 150 to 400 grits, #0000 waxed steel wool, and apply lacquer (friction-dried) as well as wax.

The finished tambootie box makes a lovely cylinder box variant.

Triple-Finned Box

Another cylinder box variant that is visually appealing happens to be a triple-finned box that looks like a British mail box. The fins may be turned tapering from top to bottom or made flush for another likable appearance. The 2-3/4 inches square x 6 inches long tulipwood stock is rough cut on the band saw to make rough turning easier. It is mounted between centers, turned to a cylinder, and 1/8 inch thick x 2 inches spigots cut at either end to fit the 2-inch O'Donnell jaws.

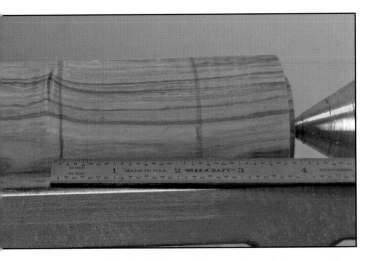

Mount the stock in the O'Donnell jaws and mark the mounting position. Draw a green pencil line 1-1/2 inches from the tailstock end and 2-1/2 inches from the first green line. This will give the proper proportion for lid and base.

Use the 1/2-inch skew with a slight rounded over arch to cut the fins. The procedure is to make a cut at 12 o'clock with the point (that is, a cut perpendicular to the lathe bed), and then an angle cut at 1 minute before 12 then 1 minute after 12. This is the classic #1 cut taught in most beginning classes. Cut at 2 minutes before 12 and then 2 minutes after 12. Continue the cuts adding minutes and make 3 grooves (1/2 groove at each end). Make sure the cuts are even and the fins are equal in thickness.

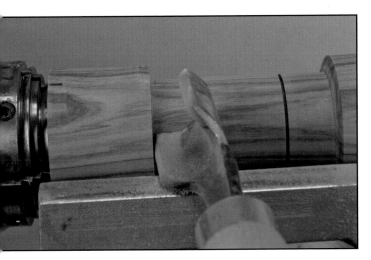

Use the narrow parting tool to cut a 1/2 inch deep groove on the two green pencil lines. Leave a 5/8 inches wide x 1/4 inch deep ring at the top of the lid. Use the roughing gouge to cut 1/4 inch deep for the desired shape. Use the rolling technique to cut at each end as demonstrated.

Continue cutting the fins until a slight taper is created. The radius difference from fin to fin is 1/16 inch. Part off the lid with the narrow parting tool.

Adjust the depth gauge so that the thickness of the lid's top will be 3/16 inches.

Use the rounded corner square-nose scraper to smooth the lid interior walls. Remember to scrape at 30 degrees off the lathe bed and use a diamond card to remove the burr as this is tulipwood, an exotic that creates catches easily.

Use the modified 1/2-inch spindle gouge to hollow out the lid.

Finish the interior by sanding with waxed sandpaper 150 to 400 grits, #0000 waxed steel wool, friction-dried lacquering, and waxing.

Cut a 1/4 inch deep x 3/32 inches wide rebate with the 1/4-inch square modified rebate tool.

Remount the base using the position marks and cut a spigot to fit the lid, as was done for the other boxes. Cut a 1/32 inch deep x 1/32 inch wide defining mark between the lid and base.

Place the lid on the base and turn off its spigot using a 3/8-inch spindle gouge.

Use the 1/2-inch skew to turn a convex top on the lid.

Finish sanding and applying the finishes to the exterior of the box.

Remove the lid and hollow out the base to a wall thickness of 3/16 inches using the modified spindle gouge.

Finish sanding and applying the finishes to the interior.

Use the narrow parting tool to cut a 1/2 inch dowel, then cut off the base using the dovetail saw. Save the unused tulipwood disc for another project.

Notice the interior of the box.

Turn a jam chuck and mount the base to finish the turning.

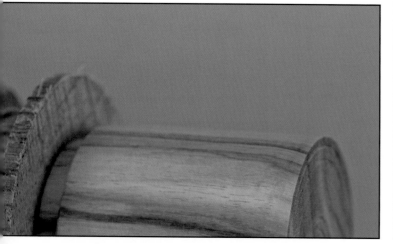

Use the skew and form a subtle concavity before applying concentric circles. Apply finishes after sanding.

The completed box has an appealing and functional look.

Chapter 3
The Classic Capsule Box

The capsule box is another classic favorite of turners that is easily constructed. Instead of having perpendicular planes, a soft, continuous curve accents the lid and base. The basic steps for its turning are the same, with a few different tools utilized for the interior curves.

The box demonstrated here is slightly larger than most boxes, but it serves a specific function. Years ago, when I first started turning boxes, my wife Susan asked for a larger box of hard wood that she could carry in her purse when traveling. The box was for her jewelry. I made an Indian rosewood box 3 inches in diameter by 5 inches tall that she still uses on her trips. The box has a few hundred thousand air miles and is no worse for wear, something that can't be said of Susan or me.

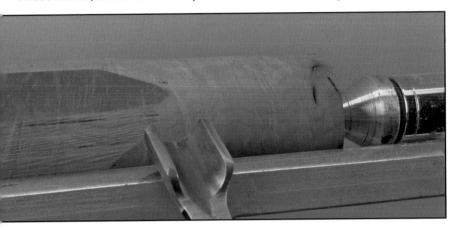

The stock selected is madrone burl that was a left over from a shipment to the Mercedes Benz factory in Germany. It seems many madrone gear shift knobs were made some years ago and the Oregon company processing madrone was about to go out of business. This gave my friend Arnie and I the opportunity to purchase, at fire sale prices, the cured dried wood blocks that had been cut into 3 x 3 inches square, variable length pieces. The selected piece is 8 inches long and has had its corners cut off on a band saw to make roughing a bit easier. The stock is mounted between centers and turned into a cylinder.

The ends are squared with a diamond parting tool.

Cut a 1/8 inch wide spigot at each end with the diamond parting tool to mount into the O'Donnell j

Measure the distance on the 2-inch O'Donnell jaws and mark it on both ends of the cylinder.

Measure 2 inches from the tailstock end and make a green circumferential pencil line. Measure 3-1/4 inches down to mark another pencil line. This will give the correct portions for lid and base, but you must remember to keep the interior depth no deeper than your fingers whenever sanding is to be attempted—an interior depth of 3 inches is my personal limit.

Use the 3/8-inch spindle gouge to cut a curvature towards the spigot.

Use a narrow parting tool to cut along the first green pencil line, creating a 1/2 inch dowel. If the tailstock is backed off the parting tool may part off the lid whenever a carefully placed hand is ready to catch it.

If you don't like the risk of catching spinning wood, use a dovetail saw to cut off the lid.

Remove the base and mount the lid in the O'Donnell jaws.

Use the 1/2-inch skew to clean up and square the lids surface.

Use the depth gauge to approximate 1/4 inch thick lid.

Use the modified hollowing tool at dead center, flute closed, to push in and drill a hole.

Continue to hollow out the lid by sweeping out to the periphery with careful cuts leaving an interior curvature.

Measure the depth of the lid.

Use a round-nose scraper to carefully smooth out the interior concavity and straighten the sides to a 1/4 inch thickness.

Mark concentric circles with the 1/2-inch skew tip

Cut a 1/4 inch deep x 1/8 inch wide rebate for the friction fit with the rebate tool.

Use waxed sandpaper, 150 to 400 grits, to sand the interior.

Use #0000 waxed steel wool to buff the sanded interior. The steel wool may be used to buff the rebate surfaces, but they should not be sanded.

Apply the 50% diluted lacquer with a soft brush and, after 30 seconds have passed, use a soft cloth to friction-dry the surface.

Apply Briwax, then buff with a soft cloth.

Remove the lid and remount the base using the position marks at the bottom and on the jaws. Measure slightly proud of the interior diameter of the lid, then, after cleaning up the surface with a skew, mark the diameter on the cut surface of the base.

Using the rebate tool cut a thin spigot to fit the lid.

When a good fit is obtained, extend the spigot to 1/4 inch.

With the narrow parting tool cut a groove 1/2 inch deep at the second green pencil line.

Use a skew to round the cylinder and begin to turn off the lid's spigot, creating a pleasant curvature.

Use the skew's point to cut concentric circles for design.

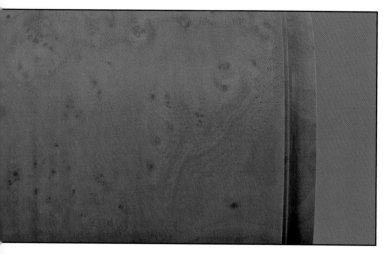

Cut a 1/32 inch deep x1/32 inch wide defining mark on the base.

With a 3/8-inch spindle gouge begin to round over the base bottom to match the curve on the lid.

Use the depth gauge to approximate the correct hollowing depth to leave a 1/4 inch wall thickness at the base.

Use the hollowing tool to hollow out the base.

Measure the depth to assure proper thickness.

Use the round-nose scraper to smooth the interior surface.

Sand the interior with waxed sandpaper 150 to 400 grits, #0000 waxed steel wool, thinned lacquer, Briwax, and then buff with a soft cloth.

Finish the exterior with sanding, applying lacquer, wax, and then polishing.

Cut with a narrow parting tool down to a 1/2 inch dowel.

Use the dovetail saw to part off the base.

Mark with dividers the interior opening of the base, cut a spigot on the remaining mounted madrone so that the base may be reverse-mounted for finishing.

Begin cutting the proper curve with the 3/8-inch spindle gouge.

Make sure the curves match after the base is turned to completion.

Cut concentric circles on the base with the 1/2-inch skew.

Complete the base's bottom by sanding with waxed sandpaper 150 to 400 grits, waxed #0000 steel wool, diluted lacquer friction dried, and then Briwax.

The interior of the finished capsule box.

The finished top and bottom of the capsule box.

The completed madrone burl capsule box designed for traveling.

Chapter 4

The Capsule Box Variants

Capsule box variants are reminiscent of cylinder box variants, but with curved surfaces. The first example is a box with a lid that looks like a bolo hat. I first saw these boxes made by Ray Key, a most expert turned box maker. The stock is highly figured Oregon walnut captured from my friend Burt's barn table stock and first used in making peppermills. Left over cut-offs oft times make the most beautiful boxes. The stock is 2-3/4 inches diameter by 5 inches long.

Mount the stock between centers after cutting off the corners. Use the roughing gouge to turn a cylinder and square the ends with a diamond parting tool. Measure a 2 inch diameter at either end and cut a 1/8 inch wide spigot for mounting in the O'Donnell jaws.

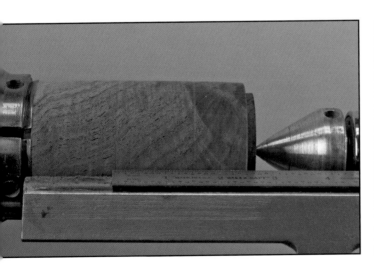

Mount the spigot in the O'Donnell jaws then make green pencil marks to define the lid and base using golden mean proportions.

Use the narrow parting tool to cut 1/2 inch deep defining lines on the green pencil marks. Next, round over the edges to the spigots.

Turn a 1/8 inch bead at the lid and base junction.

Continue to remove stock with the 3/8-inch spindle gouge to leave a 1/8 inch wide beaded rim about 3/16 inches deep.

Part off the lid and mount it in the O'Donnell jaws. Use the skew to clean up the surface and then hollow out the lid with the modified spindle gouge previously used in the other box projects. Cut concentric circles with the skew's tip after smoothing the interior surface with a round nose scraper. Cut a 1/4 inch deep x 3/32 inches wide rebate for the friction fit.

Finish the interior by sanding with waxed sandpaper 150 to 400 grits, waxed #0000 steel wool, applying diluted lacquer, and then Briwax.

Remount the base using the previously made position marks and cut a 1/4 inch spigot to fit the lid.

Mount the lid and begin turning off the spigot and rounding over the lid.

After the lid is rounded cut some concentric circles with the skew then apply the finish after sanding.

Approach the interior at a 30 degree angle to prevent catches.

Remove the lid and determine the depth needed for 3/16 inches base thickness before hollowing with the modified spindle gouge.

Finish the interior by sanding and applying the same finishes as for the lid.

Use a 3/8-inch square steel round-nose scrapper to smooth the inside shape of the box.

Remount the lid and apply the finishing touches.

Apply the finishing wax.

Part off the base and mount it in a jam chuck. Save the left over stock for another project.

Reverse mount the base in the turned jam chuck to round over the bottom.

Compare the lid curvature to match the base.

Turn the base to completion, sand, and then apply finishes.

The completed box makes a lovely container with a rim that allows easy gripping for lid removal.

Decorated Capsule Box

Simple squat capsule boxes make desirable objects when decorated by a chatter tool. The use of a chatter tool is easy if held properly and if very dense exotics are used as the stock. The box demonstrated is made from spalted English boxwood. The capsule box is turned just like the first described capsule box, only shorter.

A nifty chatter tool give to me by my friend Eli Avisera is used to make the defining marks. As one loosens the set screw and extends the blade more chatter is created. Basically, the tool vibrates against the wood by transferred harmonics. A similar spiral is often time produced by tools held too firmly against the rotating stock.

After the lid's exterior and interior surfaces are turned to completion, except for lacquer and wax, the chatter tool may be applied. Turn the lathe down to 1000 rpms and rotate the tool about 45 degrees on the tool rest (if one uses the point of the tool a nasty pitted, irregular pattern will ensue). Use the side of the blade with light pressure to the left of the center point. Apply the tool to the left of a clear spot and notice the nifty appearance.

Use the tip of the skew chisel to cut defining lines in the lid's interior.

Some turners leave the chatter work plain but I prefer to apply the diluted lacquer and then polish with wax to give a pleasant appearance.

Remove the lid and remount the base. Turn a spigot to fit the lid and then turn to completion with sanding. Next apply the chatter tool to create designs.

Remember to turn down the speed and apply the tool using the side of the blade with light pressure.

Use the chatter tool to make several rings and then define their borders with the tip of the skew.

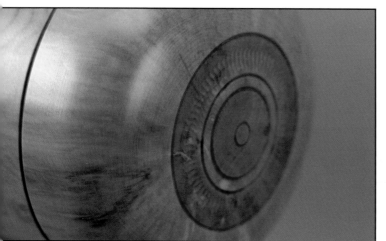

Apply the lacquer and wax for a lovely finished effect.

Hollow the base, use the thin round-nose scrapper to smooth the walls, and then sand to completion. Apply the chatter tool to the bottom of the base. Finish with lacquer and wax.

Part off the base, reverse chuck it on a jam chuck, and finish rounding off the bottom. Sand to completion and then apply chatter work as was previously done. Apply lacquer and wax.

Completed capsule box with chatter work.

Chatter work on the interior.

Chatter work on the top and bottom.

Chapter 5
The Raffan Type Boxes

The Raffan type box is an interestingly shaped box that defies the proportions of the golden mean but still appears very functional and visually pleasing. Its subtly tapered base helps offset its thinner lid. This box is favored by women because the lid is easily removed by the rim to reveal a larger compartment than found in conventional boxes. The timber used here is a figured myrtle, a prized turner's wood found along the Oregon coast.

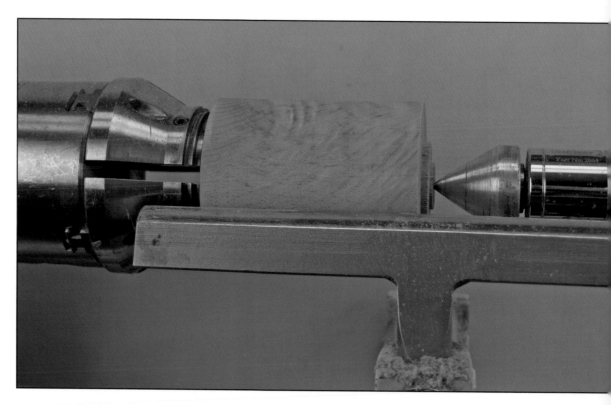

After securing the 3 x 3 x 5 inch stock between centers, roughing out a cylinder, squaring the ends, and turning 1-1/2 inch spigots at either end, mount the stock in the O'Donnell jaws.

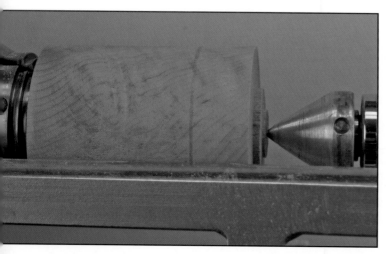

Mark a green pencil line a little less than 1/3 the distance from the tailstock end.

Cut to a depth of 3/16 inches with a narrow parting tool to define the lid's rim. Remove stock from the lid to the 3/16 inches cut. Part off the lid.

Taper the base towards the headstock by about 1/2 inch, using the roughing gouge and rolling cuts whenever the jaws are approached.

Mark the position pencil lines for remounting then remove the base.

Mount the lid and clean up the cut surface with a 1/2-inch skew.

Begin hollowing out the lid, using the modified spindle gouge, but leave a center pointed nipple (ultimately this adds support to the lid whenever the lid is thinned).

Use a round-nose scrapper to smooth the interior.

Cut a 1/4 inch deep, 3/32 inches wide rebate with the rebate tool.

Apply concentric circle cuts with the tip of the skew

Sand the lid to completion, apply diluted lacquer, and then wax.

Remove the lid and remount the base using the position marks as guides. With dividers measuring slightly proud of the lid's opening diameter, mark a guide template for the spigot. Cut a 1/4 inch wide spigot to fit the lid.

Press on the lid after turning the base the exact diameter of the lid's portion above the rim.

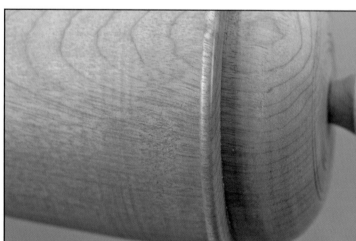

Turn off the spigot of the lid and form a tapered knob with a blunted rim. Use the skew to cut concentric circles on the knob as well as the lid.

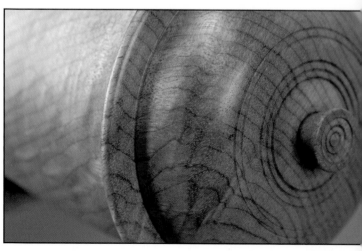

Finish the lid by sanding and applying the lacquer and wax.

Remove the lid and hollow out the base using the modified spindle gouge.

Turn a subtle curve on the bottom, then finish with a round-nose scrapper. Sand and apply lacquer and then wax.

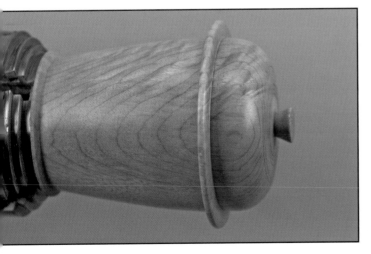

Complete the exterior of the base by sanding, applying lacquer, and then waxing. Part off the base by using a narrow parting tool to create a 1/2 inch dowel and then use the dove-tail saw to remove the base.

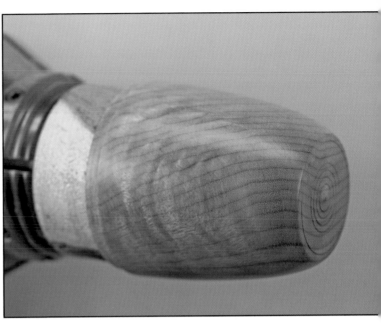

Turn a jam chuck to fit the base. Turn the base to completion, sanding and applying finishes.

Completed exterior of the Raffan box.

Chapter 6

The Pagoda Box

As far as I know, the pagoda box is a creation of Ray Key. Searching wide and far has yielded no other inventor; so to escape accusations of pastiche or sciolism I give full credit to Ray and display my modifications in the pagoda box's construction. The motif behind the pagoda box is a stacked series of boxes that blend into one another as a whole. The rim of the "coolie hat" lid should extend to the diameter of the base box's bottom. Each successive box should be progressive larger in diameter than its overhead companion and present a subtle side flare of its walls. The compartment numbers may be as few as 3 or as many as 9 depending on the patience and expertise of the turner. One must be very careful in construction so that the bottom discs of the serially turned stacked boxes don't become too thin and fracture. Due to the time (about 2-3 hours) and accuracy involved the turner must pay attention to every detail in the instructions

and construction. A very dense timber makes the best box, but I've succumbed to Alaska birch on occasion with remarkably good results. If one wishes a wonderfully visually appealing project the pagoda box will fit the bill.

The selected 3 inches square x 6-1/2 inches stock is marblewood, a most dense timber with properties similar to stone. It is not quite as hard as blackwood but fairly close. Its marbled appearance of purple veins serpiginously woven throughout the tan fibers is most interesting. As with the other stock pieces, the corners have been carefully cut off on a band saw, the timber mounted between centers and turned to a smooth cylinder with a roughing gouge, the ends squared with a diamond parting tool, 1-1/2 inches x 1/8 inch spigots turned at each end, and then mounted in the O'Donnell jaws of the Axminster chuck. The compartment size selected is 1 inch except for the coolie hat lid which is 1-1/4 inches.

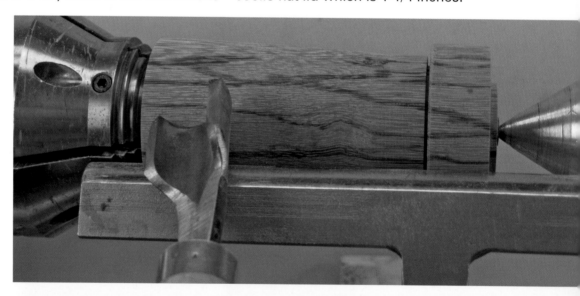

After the circumferential pencil mark is made 1-1/4 inches from the tailstock end, make a 1/4 inch deep cut with the narrow parting tool along the pencil line.
Use the roughing gouge to taper from the headstock end to the base of the parting tool cut. Use the roll-over technique towards the chuck jaws and tailstock 1-1/4 inch spigot.

Use the 3/8-inch spindle gouge to cut a taper towards the spigot at the tailstock.

38

Draw a pencil line 1 inch to the left of the parting tool cut.

Remove the base after marking its mounted position on the wood. Remount the lid in the O'Donnell jaws. Clean up the cut marks with the 1/2-inch skew, then mark with dividers a circumferential ring, 3/16 inches less in diameter than the top of the first compartment (the wall thickness will be 3/16 inches, so that the spigot size must be 3/32 inches thick).

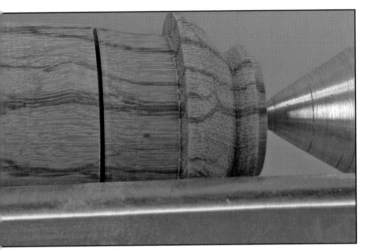

Cut a 1/4 inch deep groove with the narrow parting tool.

Begin to hollow out the lid with the modified spindle gouge. Make sure the divider marks are intact.

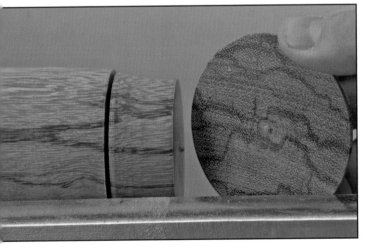

Part off the top lid and turn a subtle taper to the top compartment.

Approximate the depth needed to make the wall thickness 3/16 inches and check with the depth gauge.

Use the 3/8-inch round-nose scraper at a 30 degree angle to smooth out the interior.

Use the 1/4-inch rebate tool to cut a 1/4 inch deep rebate at the divider marks. There should be enough material so that one doesn't cut through the tapered lid with the rebate tool.

Sand with waxed sandpaper 150 to 400 grits, #0000 waxed steel wool, apply diluted lacquer, friction dry, and then apply Briwax and polish.

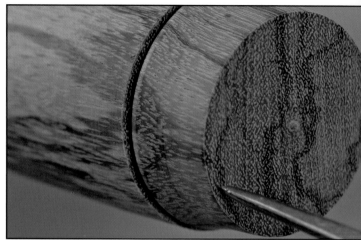

Measure slightly proud of the inside opening of the lid and mark the distance on the cut skew cleaned surface of the base.

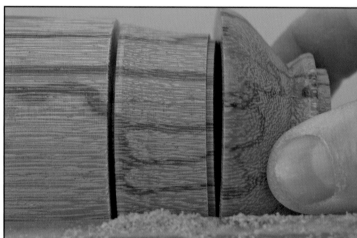

Cut a narrow spigot until a firm fit is established and then extend the spigot to 1/4 inch to fit the lid.

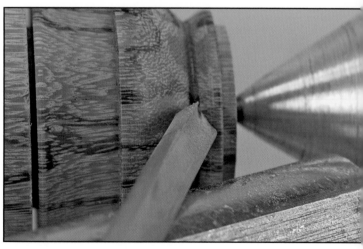

Place the lid on the base and bring up the tailstock to begin shaping the coolie hat.

Remove the tailstock and finish the turning to a soft point.

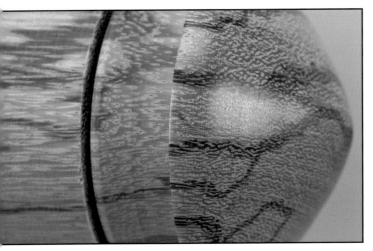

Sand with waxed sandpaper 150 to 400 grits, #0000 waxed steel wool, apply diluted lacquer, friction dry, and then apply Briwax and polish.

Approximate the depth needed for the first container. Remember there needs to be a 1/4 inch rebate in the bottom of this container and a bottom thickness of 3/16 inches. That will leave a depth of 9/16 inches.

Use the modified 1/2-inch hollowing gouge to create a flat bottom, curved wall interior. Use the round nose scrapper to smooth the base and walls.

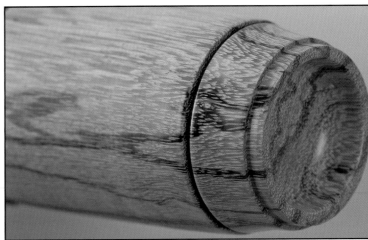

Sand to completion, lacquer, and apply wax on both interior and exterior. Don't sand the friction-fitted spigot.

Measure 1 inch down from the finished compartment.

Use the narrow parting tool to cut a groove 1/4 inch deep and then cut a groove at the bottom of the finished compartment, leaving a 1/2 inch dowel. Turn a subtle curve on the second compartment tapering to the first compartment.

Mount the first compartment and clean up the cut marks on the bottom with a skew.

Use the dovetail saw to cut off the first compartment and remove the base stock.

Measure the top diameter of compartment #2 minus slightly less than 3/16 inches and mark it on the bottom of compartment #1.

Mount a piece of scrap stock in the O'Donnell jaws and turn a jam chuck to hold the first compartment by its spigot.

Use the modified spindle gouge to hollow out a 1/4 inch deep cavity. Clean the bottom surface with a square nose scrapper.

Use the 1/4 inch square rebate tool to cut a 1/4 inch deep rebate.

Check the square of the cut with calipers.

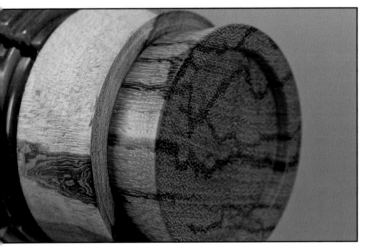

Sand, lacquer, and wax the finished bottom. Don't sand the friction fitted area.

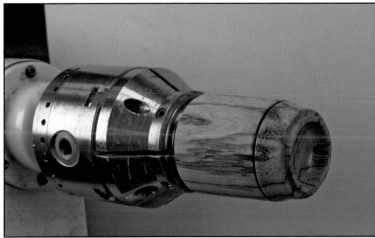

Remount the base using the position pencil marks and turn a spigot on compartment #2 to fit the base of compartment #1. Hollow out the interior of compartment #2 just as was done for compartment #1 and finish by sanding, lacquering, and waxing both interior and exterior, but don't sand the spigot.

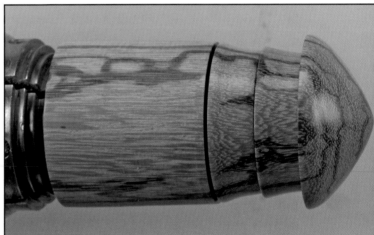

Check the fit of the three finished pieces before proceeding.

Remove the finished pieces then measure 1 inch down towards the headstock end and make a 1/4 inch deep cut with the narrow parting tool.

Turn a slight taper towards the #2 compartment base and part off compartment #2. Remove the base from the chuck.

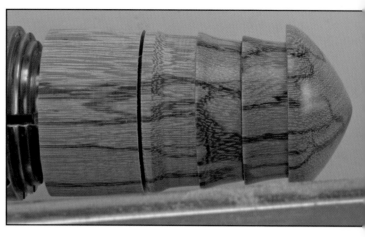

Remount the base using the position pencil marks, turn a spigot to fit the bottom of compartment #2 and check the fit of all compartments.

Use the same jam chuck for compartment #2 as for #1—remember, the taper diameter is slightly larger with each successive compartment so that the same jam chuck may be used by opening the rebate only slightly with the rebate tool.

Remove the finished compartments and then complete compartment #3 by hollowing it out, scrapping it smooth, sanding interior and exterior surfaces, applying lacquer, and then waxing. Before parting off compartment #3, measure 1 inch towards the headstock and cut a 1/4 inch deep groove with the narrow parting tool. Cut a subtle taper towards compartment #3 and then part off compartment #3 using the dovetail saw for the final separation.

Mount compartment #2 in the jam chuck and turn it to completion and finish as was accomplished for compartment #1.

Cut a rebate to fit compartment #3 in the jam chuck. Turn the base of compartment #3 to completion as was done for the other compartments, sand, lacquer, and wax.

Replace the base utilizing the pencil position marks on the O'Donnell jaws and then turn a spigot on compartment #4 to fit the base of compartment #3.

Finish the bottom of compartment #4 with concentric circles made with the skew, sand, lacquer, and then wax. Remove the finished compartment and assemble the pagoda box.

Turn compartment #4 to completion, sand, lacquer, and then wax. Part off compartment #4 as was done for the other compartments.

Finished pagoda box displaying all compartments and the lid.

Widen the rebate in the jam chuck for compartment #4 and mount it in the chuck. Finish the bottom with the 1/2-inch skew making a subtle concavity.

Finished pagoda box of marblewood fitted together.

Chapter 7
The Clam Shell Box

A wonderful small container to make out of left-over timber is the clam shell box. All one really needs is a piece of turned wood about 1-1/2 inches thick. If one notes the left over pieces of the various boxes described herein and looks in the gallery one will find completed clam shell boxes of those particular pieces. The only difference in the clam shell box is in the lid; instead of having a female fitting it has a male fitting. This is because of the shallow arc of the lid prohibits cutting an adequate rebate to hold a spigot of the base. As a consequence the fittings are reversed, requiring another step in chucking. The same proportions of lid to base (golden mean) are utilized and the same procedures in turning are used. Sometimes a foot is turned on the box and at other times, when the stock is thinner, none is placed.

The left over stock from the bolo hat capsule box is mounted in the O'Donnell jaws by the previous position pencil marks. A 1/8 inch wide spigot to fit the 1-1/2-inch jaws has been turned on the cut end (tailstock side).

Use the narrow (1/16 inch wide) parting tool to cut a groove 1/2 inch deep and then begin cutting a curve from the first pencil line towards the tailstock spigot. Part off the lid and remove the base from the chuck.

With a green pencil mark a circumferential line 1/2 inch from the tailstock end and another line 1/4 inch towards the head-stock end on this 1-1/2 inch thick stock. The latter line will be the cut line to separate the box and the former will be the spigot distance to be cut later.

Mount the lid in the chuck and cut a 3/16 inches deep x 3/16 inches wide spigot. Clean up the parted surface with the 1/2-inch skew.

Use the modified spindle gouge to hollow out the lid to a 3/16 inches thickness. Note: With the thinness of the lid and experience of making the other boxes one may eyeball the measurement if one feels comfortable in so doing.

Use the round-nose scrapper to smooth out the interior.

Sand all surfaces except the spigot with waxed sandpaper 150 to 400 grits and #0000 waxed steel wool, apply diluted lacquer, friction dry, apply Briwax and then polish. Note: Lacquer and wax are to be applied to the spigot. Also note that a very subtle round-over of the lid's edge needs to be made for definition and easy opening of the box.

Remove the lid and remount the base using the position pencil marks. Using dividers, mark a circle slightly shy of the lid spigot diameter on the cut cleaned surface of the base. Hollow out the base with the hollowing tool.

Use the round nose scrapper to smooth the base interior.

Recheck the spigot distance with the dividers.

Use the rebate tool to cut a 3/16 inches deep fitting for the lid.

Mount the lid and begin to turn off the spigot.

Complete the arc so that a smooth flowing convexity results. Complete the arc on the base to the jaws.

Sand, lacquer, and wax to completion both lid and base. Remove the lid and do the same for the interior of the base. Remember to sand over a subtle curve on the bases edge for definition.

Remove the base and turn a jam chuck of soft wood to fit the base.

Begin to turn off the spigot to form a foot at the end of the smooth curve.

Use the skew to place concentric circles on the foot and complete by sanding, lacquering, and waxing.

The finished capsule box makes a lovely container rescued from throw away timber.

Chapter 8
The Gourd Box

The gourd or pumpkin box was first brought to my attention by Stuart Batty during one of his several trips to Alaska. Even though it looks more like a gourd than a pumpkin Stuart still refers to it as the latter—I guess I'll never understand the British. The gourd happens to be one of my wife's favorite boxes and every time I make one from new timber it ends up in her collection.

The gourd box has a male fitting (spigot) lid as does the clam shell box. The reasons are the same, that is, the ogee arc prohibits cutting a rebate for a spigot without going through the lid.

In constructing the box at least 4 inches square stock is needed so that a pleasing squat appearance may be had. The box is hollowed using the modified spindle gouge as well as a curved hollowing tool like that used in hollowing globes for Christmas ornaments in *7 Great Turning Projects for The Smaller Lathe* published by Schiffer.

The stock selected is Afzelia burl 4 X 4 X 5-1/2 inches. As was done before, the corners were cut off on a band saw to create a somewhat cylindrical appearing stock. It was mounted between centers and turned to a cylinder with the roughing gouge, ends squared with the diamond parting tool, and then a 1-1/2 inches diameter x 1/8 inch wide spigot turned at each end to fit the O'Donnell jaws of the Axminster chuck.

Mount the stock in the O'Donnell jaws and, with the tailstock brought up, turn the cylinder true.

Measure 2 inches from the tailstock end and draw a pencil line.

Use the narrow parting tool to cut a 3/4 inches deep groove.

Use the roughing gouge to cut a smooth taper from the top third of the base towards the tailstock end.

Use the 1/4-inch rebate tool to cut a 1/4 inch spigot above the parting tool cut, so that a 2 inch diameter spigot is created. One can use curved dividers to check the proper diameter.

Begin shaping a 1/2 inch deep x 1/8 inch ring above the spigot with a round over bead. The diameter of the ring is about 3 inches. Also begin turning an ogee form leaving about a 1/2 inch wide area for the top knob. The spigot for mounting should be left intact.

Form a bulbous area at the base of the bottom section with another subtle ogee tapering to the foot area. Turn the junction of the base to lid so that an appearance of a flowing transition may be appreciated. Remember to mark position marks on the base for remounting.

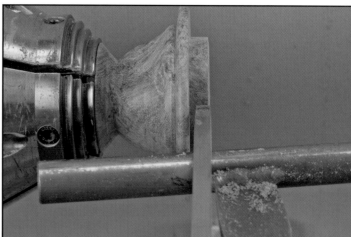

Part off the lid and remove the base from the chuck. Remount the lid and square the spigot with the 1/4-inch rebate tool. Clean up the cut edges of the ring and the spigot bottom with the skew.

Hollow out the lid.

Use the depth gauge to estimate how deep the hole needs to be to give a wall thickness of 3/16 inches.

Use the 3/8-inch round-nose scrapper to smooth out the lid interior.

Sand with waxed sandpaper 150 to 400 grits, #0000 waxed steel wool, apply diluted lacquer, friction dry, apply Briwax, and polish.

Remove the lid and remount the base using the pencil position marks previously made. With dividers, mark a cut ring slightly shy of the lid spigot diameter. Partially hollow the base, being careful not to cut to the marked ring. Use the 1/4-inch rebate tool to cut the fitting.

Continue to hollow to the depth of 3/16 inches for the base and foot, sweeping out with the hollowing tool as far as the neck constriction will allow.

Use the rebate tool to cut an interior sleeve until a perfect tight fit is obtained for the lid.

Complete the ogee on the lid and turn a tapered nubbin. Flute the nubbin's edge and cut concentric circles with the skew on its top. Sand, lacquer, and wax the lid to a finish.

Use the skew to turn a subtle concavity in the foot and place some concentric circles for design. Sand, lacquer, and wax to completion.

Remove the lid and use the curved small hollowing tool to round out the squat interior of the base. Use a round nose scrapper to smooth the base and sides. Sand, lacquer, and wax to completion.

The completed Afzelia burl gourd box will no doubt end up in my wife's collection.

Remove the base and turn a jam chuck to reverse mount the base so that the ogee may be continued into the base.

Chapter 9
The Bottle Top and Finial Top Boxes

Bottle top and finial top boxes are another creation of Ray Key. They remind me of the poor man's hollow form. The construction of the bottle top box is not difficult and during the construction the base is used as the jam chuck to hold the lid while its underside is turned and decorated. The same may be said of the finial top box as well. The form of the bottle top reminds me of an upside down brandy snifter. If one sticks to that form a perfect box will be made every time. An advantage of the bottle top box is that someone with arthritic hands may easily open the box; consequently, the bottle top form is great for drawer knobs, threaded tops

for reliquaries, or any other fixture requiring a compromised grip.

The stock selected for this project is teak burl. One should wear a mask or respirator whenever turning teak (especially if it is green) because the vaporized oils are rather irritating to the respiratory tree. Nevertheless, one may taste teak for several days after working in the shop with the wood.

The 3 x 3 x 5 inches stock has had its corners cut off on a band saw, turned to a cylinder between centers with the roughing gouge, the ends squared with a diamond parting tool, 1-1/2 inches by 1/8 inch spigots turned at either end, and then mounted in the O'Donnell jaws of an Axminster chuck.

After mounting the stock re-turn the cylinder if any wobble is noted. Measure up 3 inches from the base and draw a pencil line for separation of the lid and base.

Use the narrow parting tool to cut a 3/4 inches deep groove and begin removing stock with the 3/8-inch spindle gouge.

Begin shaping the bottle top leaving a 1/2 inch wide spigot with a little greater than 1 inch diameter. Turn a broad cove leaving a 3/16 inches spigot at the end.

Measure with calipers to assure the tailstock spigot is about 1/8 inch less in diameter than the 1/2 inch wide spigot.

Turn a subtle concavity on the top and make concentric circles for design with the skew after removing the tailstock.

Round over the base then part off the lid using the narrow parting tool.

Measure the top with calipers or dividers.

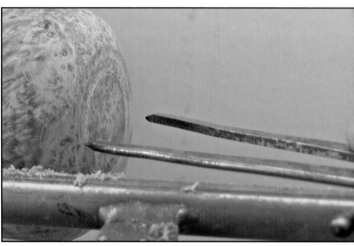

Mark a circle on the base slightly shy of the measured top.

54

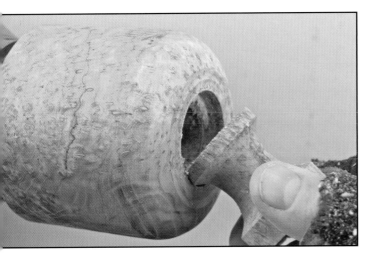

Begin to hollow out the base using the 1/2-inch modified spindle gouge. Be careful not to hollow to the marked circle.

Use the 1/4-inch rebate tool to cut a 1/8 inch recess to fit the lids top. The fit should be quite tight as the extended bottom of the lid will be finished by this fitting.

Turn a subtle concavity and cut concentric circles with the tip of the skew. Finish the bottom by sanding, and applying lacquer and then Briwax, as was done on previous projects.

Remove the lid and measure the bottom portion. Transfer the divider marks slightly shy of the lids bottom measurement. Use the rebate tool to cut a firm fit.

Place the bottle top in its fitting. The tailstock end of the bottom fitted lid will extend above the base. Begin shaping the lid using careful cuts with the 3/8-inch spindle gouge.

Finish forming a transition from the top of the base curvature to the bottom of the lid so that no defect is visible. Slightly taper the top to the stem so that a continuous curve is created. Taper the base towards the headstock with the 3/8-inch spindle gouge so a brandy glass form is created.

Use the small curved hollowing tool to reach the inside shoulders. After hollowing is complete sand with waxed sandpaper 150 to 400 grits, #0000 waxed steel wool, apply diluted lacquer, friction dry, and then apply Briwax.

Sand all surfaces to completion, lacquer all sanded parts, apply Briwax and then polish with a soft cloth.

Turn a double spigot jam chuck out of scrap wood to fit the reversed base.

Remove the lid and finish hollowing out the base with the modified spindle gouge. Remember to measure the depth so that the thickness is about 3/16 inches. Also remember to leave a narrow shelf for the lid to rest on.

Mount the base and finish turning the spigot off the bottom.

Finial Top Box

Make some concentric circles on the base for design and finish by sanding, lacquering, and waxing.

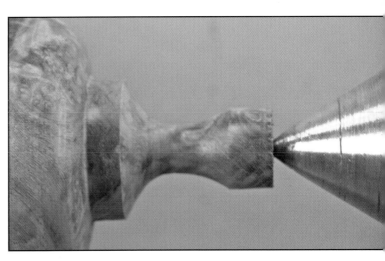

The finial top box is turned exactly like the bottle top box, except that the distal end of the box (tailstock end) has a spigot about 5/8 inches wide and 5/8 inches in diameter.

The finished box presents a visually appealing piece.

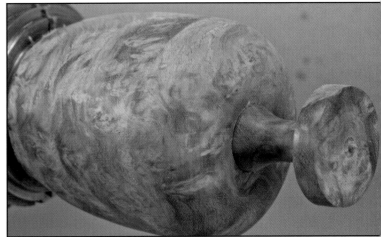

The opening in the base is made to fit the 5/8 inches spigot so that the lid's base may be turned, decorated, and then finished before broadening the opening to fit the lid's base.

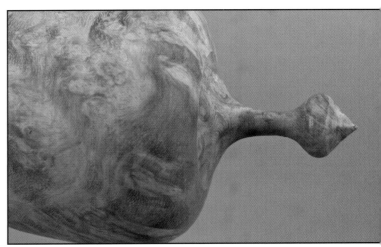

The lid is fitted on and a finial is turned. Some might like to make shorter finials or use other forms of artistic license. Remove the lid and finish the interior as was accomplished for the bottle top box.

The Gallery

Pagoda boxes. Back row left to right: Alaska birch, Ceylon satinwood; front row left to right: marblewood, Gaboon ebony.

Grouping of Raffan boxes. Back row left to right: curly myrtle classic Raffan box, modified Raffan box of koa; front row left to right: squat Raffan box of madrone burl that houses a music box, and a large curly redwood Raffan box.

Grouping of gourd type boxes. Back row left to right: English hawthorn, Russian olive burl, curly maple burl, Afzelia burl; front row left to right: madrone burl, zebrawood, Ceylon satinwood, and Spanish olivewood.

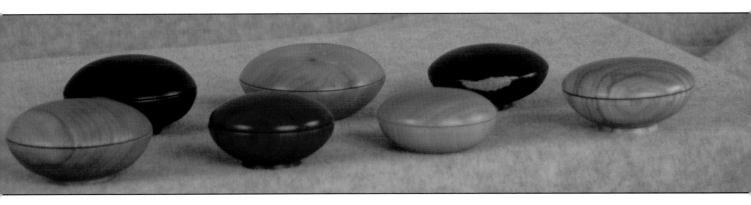

Collection of clam shell boxes, some with a foot and others without, made from left over or scrap timber from previously turned stock for boxes. Left to right: figured walnut, Gaboon ebony, violet rosewood, madrone burl, pink ivory, Mexican kingwood, and tulipwood.

Several cylinder type boxes. Left to right back row: tapered fin type cylinder box of tulipwood, Swiss pear cylinder box, ring rimmed tambootie cylinder box, straight fin violet rosewood cylinder box; front row left to right: curly maple cylinder box, small pink ivory cylinder box with chatter work on its lid, and amboyna burl cylinder box.

Lens boxes of maple burl and a blackwood lid with accent wood of coco bolo; walnut and a blackwood lid with accent wood of holly; and walnut burl and a maple burl lid with accent wood of holly. These boxes are another Hans Weissflog invention requiring about 35 different steps and multiple chucking tasks to turn to completion.

Collection of capsule type boxes. Back row left to right: classic travel capsule box of madrone burl, bolo hat type capsule box of figured walnut, large travel capsule box of madrone burl, small egg shaped rimmed capsule box of tulipwood, coolie hat type box with chatter work on lid of figured myrtle; front row left to right: boxwood capsule box with chatter work, elongated egg capsule box of myrtle burl, coolie hat type box of satinwood showing hollow form appearance and male type fitting lid, and small pink ivory capsule box with chatter work.

Unusual boxes. Back row left to right: Saturn box of Masur birch with lid removed, Saturn box of mesquite (the rings for these boxes are cut from either side with a specially ground tool point so that the entire ring rotates—a Hans Weissflog invention); front: spherical Spanish olivewood box on an African blackwood pedestal.

Bottle top and finial top boxes. Back row left to right: amboyna burl elongated finial top box, teak burl bottle top box, violet rosewood bottle top box; front row left to right: African blackwood short finial top box, and marblewood bottle top box. Notice how the hollow form boxes look like upside down brandy snifters.

Blackwood boxes. The two on either side have two rotating rings that are cut from either side of the lid as was accomplished with the Saturn boxes. African blackwood with sap wood is utilized to give greater appreciation of the rings and the pseudo appearance of yin and yang. The center box has had its inset made from a sphere of holly turning grooves in two perpendicular planes and cutting off the intersection to glue into an opening in the lid. The underside is then turned smooth with a 3/8-inch spindle gouge, and concentric circles added for decoration. Both of these type boxes are Weissflog ideas.

Boxes with extremely thin twisted finials. Back row left to right: Putumuju, red lace; front row left to right: tulipwood with an egg shape and captive ring on the foot, English boxwood, and tulipwood. These are the types of boxes Stuart Mortimer produces.

Pierced-through lidded boxes of boxwood and blackwood. The piercing is accomplished using a very narrow, thinly ground, high speed steel cutter. The top circles are first cut off center, then the undersides of the lids are cut on center. The thickness of the cuts is 1-1/2 mm so that an exact lid thickness of 3 mm is absolutely necessary. The center box's lid is turned on 3 different axes, 120 degrees apart. This technique is another Weissflog conception.

Transilluminated lid of the center box from the previous photo showing the intricate pattern produced.

Acknowledgments

Firstly, I should like to acknowledge and thank the great mentors who taught me how to make boxes. Several classes with Ray Key yielded many ideas in this book. Even though my own modifications were applied, many of the boxes are Key inventions. Stuart Batty has been instrumental in his teaching of perfection and detail in making not only cylinder boxes, but the gourd (pumpkin in British) box. Richard Raffan has been helpful and is well known for his signature box shared among the many students he has instructed over the years. And finally, I should like to thank Hans Weissflog for his instruction on how to make the Saturn, pierced-through, lens, rotating ring, and complicated form boxes. Even though no chapters were included on constructing his signature works there are samples in the gallery. And last but not least, I should like to thank Arnie Geiger, whose insistence on my taking advanced classes has been instrumental to my success as a wood turner.

I owe many thanks to my wife, Susan, who is quite tolerant of my absence when turning, teaching, and typing. Her support for 38 years has been invaluable and much appreciated.

Many thanks go to Doug Congdon-Martin for his editing of this book as well as others. He certainly makes the entire process painless. Finally, I should like to thank Peter and Pete Schiffer, my publisher and marketing gurus, for their support and tremendous latitude in creating this text.